eBAY

ABDO
Publishing Company

TECHNOLOGY
PIONEERS

eBAy

THE COMPANY AND ITS FOUNDER

by Martin Gitlin

Content Consultant
Nora Paul
Director of the Institute for New Media Studies
University of Minnesota

CREDITS

Published by ABDO Publishing Company, 8000 West 78th Street, Edina, Minnesota 55439. Copyright © 2011 by Abdo Consulting Group, Inc. International copyrights reserved in all countries. No part of this book may be reproduced in any form without written permission from the publisher. The Essential Library™ is a trademark and logo of ABDO Publishing Company.

Printed in the United States of America,
North Mankato, Minnesota
112010
012011

 THIS BOOK CONTAINS AT LEAST 10% RECYCLED MATERIALS.

Editor: Karen Latchana Kenney
Copy Editor: Beth Townsend
Interior Design and Production: Emily Love
Cover Design: Emily Love

Library of Congress Cataloging-in-Publication Data
Gitlin, Marty.
  eBay : the company and its founder / by Martin Gitlin.
     p. cm. -- (Technology pioneers)
  Includes bibliographical references and index.
  ISBN 978-1-61714-807-1
  1. Omidyar, Pierre, 1967---Juvenile literature. 2. Executives-
-United States--Biography--Juvenile literature. 3. Business
people--United States--Biography--Juvenile literature. 4. eBay
(Firm)--History--Juvenile literature. 5. Internet auctions--Juvenile
literature. I. Title.
  HC102.5.O48G58 2011
  381'.177092--dc22
  [B]
                                              2010044663

TABLE OF CONTENTS

Pierre Omidyar could not predict in 1996 how successful
his Web site would become in the future.

BIRTH OF A GIANT

L abor Day weekend was fast approaching. With
three days off from work, many people living
near San Francisco planned to enjoy the sights
and sounds of the beautiful and vibrant Northern
California city—but not Pierre Omidyar. The only

sight he would be seeing was his computer screen; the only sound he would hear would be the tap of keys on his keyboard. He had big plans, but they did not include leaving his small town house.

It was 1995, and Omidyar was working on creating an online auction site. The World Wide Web had rapidly been gaining users. Eventually millions of Americans would be able to connect just by using their computers and the Internet.

CATEGORIES

When Omidyar started AuctionWeb, he was not sure what people would want to buy and sell. So he created categories for items he thought would be useful for customers. The first categories included Antiques and Collectibles, Computer Hardware and Software, Consumer Electronics, Books and Comics, Automotive, and Miscellaneous.

The 28-year-old spent that Friday, September 1, in the extra bedroom he had converted into a home office. He named the site he was building AuctionWeb. By Labor Day it was completed. It was functional, but certainly not pleasing to look at. The blue-black lettering against the gray background was ugly. The idea was brilliant, though. It allowed people to buy or sell items online.

Several twists made AuctionWeb appealing and unique. For the first time, buyers could shop for just about anything they wanted in one spot. No longer did they have to travel to several stores and compare prices before making a purchase. In addition, the auction setup allowed sellers to take the highest bid for an item, which maximized their earning potential. And, in the beginning, it was a free service for both buyers and sellers.

NOT MOTIVATED BY MONEY

AuctionWeb was merely a hobby for Omidyar. Turning the largest possible profit did not motivate him. He embraced opportunities to solve new problems and find ways to help people do business. That core philosophy has remained with Omidyar. He explained,

PEDDLING PEZ

As Omidyar's business grew, so did a rumor about how it started. While it may have only been a public relations campaign, word spread that Omidyar launched AuctionWeb to sell fiancée Pam Wesley's vintage PEZ Candy dispenser collection.

PEZ Candy was created in Vienna, Austria, in 1927. In 1949, the small mint candies were packaged in a dispenser. In the 1950s, more flavors and dispensers were added to make the candy appealing to American children. Some early dispensers included robots and Santas, and later famous cartoon characters. When certain dispensers were discontinued, their value increased. PEZ dispensers have since become valuable collector's items.

The desire to sell PEZ dispensers may have been part of Omidyar's inspiration for an auction Web site, but he had been thinking about it for a while. Pam, however, never wanted to be remembered as a PEZ dispenser collector. Omidyar explained her side of the story:

> Whenever she hears about it she rolls her eyes. [She says,] "Tell them I'm a management consultant. Tell them I have a master's degree in molecular biology. I am not just this little Pez candy collector."[1]

I've got a passion for solving a problem that I think I can solve in a new way. And that maybe it helps that nobody has done it before as well. . . . You know, there's a sense of pride of doing something brand new, and I'm particularly inspired by problems that seem easily solvable. . . . And so with eBay [then AuctionWeb], the whole idea there was just to help people do business with one another on the Internet. And people thought it was impossible because how could people on the Internet—remember this is 1995—how could they trust each other? How could they get to know each other? And I thought that was silly. You know, it was a silly concern because people are basically good, honest people. So that was very motivating. It was "Gee, I'll just do it. I'll just show them. Let's see what happens."[2]

Not one person visited Omidyar's new site that Labor Day. He ran AuctionWeb from home using an existing Internet account for which he paid just $30 a month. To save money, Omidyar linked the new Web site with an existing site he had created for his consulting and technology business, Echo Bay Technology Group. The Web address for that business was ebay.com.

Omidyar did make some small attempts to publicize AuctionWeb. The day he launched the site, he placed an announcement on one Web site and a small ad on another. They read, "Run an auction or join the fun of an existing auction."[3] The problem was that the announcement did not run until the day after AuctionWeb went live, and the ad did not appear for weeks. It seemed that the only person who knew about AuctionWeb was Omidyar.

Omidyar continued to post announcements about the site and soon word started to spread. Successful sellers and bidders, especially those who bought and sold computer equipment, began e-mailing others about the wonders of AuctionWeb. By the end of the year, thousands of auctions had been hosted on the site, and approximately 10,000 bids had been placed.

NO LONGER FREE

At the beginning of 1996, the site was receiving so many visitors it was slowing down the system of the company that provided Omidyar's

ENVELOPE OVERLOAD

After Omidyar started charging sellers on his auction Web site, the small amounts of money that arrived at his home came in every imaginable form. Some people taped coins to index cards. Others shoved crumpled dollar bills into envelopes. Still others wrote checks for tiny amounts.

As AuctionWeb gained in popularity, envelopes containing customer payments piled up in Omidyar's home.

Internet service. The company responded by raising his monthly fee from $30 to $250, the rate it charged for businesses. Because of this cost increase, Omidyar felt he had no choice but to start charging fees on AuctionWeb.

Omidyar decided to keep the service free for buyers in the belief that charging them would reduce their number and the amount of activity on the site. He also decided not to charge sellers to list items but to take part of the final price of each item that was sold. He set the fees at 5 percent of the sale price for items below $25 and at 2.5 percent of the price for items above that figure.

PAYPAL

PayPal began in 1999 and provided a service that made Internet shopping safe and easy. The PayPal site allows buyers to store credit information on the site. When a buyer wants to purchase something, he or she can pay using a PayPal account. This keeps the buyer's credit information safe, because the buyer is not entering account numbers on different and possibly unprotected Web sites. Omidyar purchased the company for $1.5 billion in 2002.

Then he crossed his fingers. Would people continue to sell on AuctionWeb? He feared his entire concept would fail. But he did have one advantage over most actual stores. He did not need to rent a warehouse to hold the items bought and sold. Omidyar had no warehouse, because everything up for sale remained in the hands of the buyers and sellers. Omidyar had no storage or shipping costs—what he was providing was the technology to run a matching service for those who had something to sell and the people who might want to buy it.

Since Internet technology had not reached the point in which payments could be made online, buyers sent money directly to Omidyar. Stacks of envelopes holding checks and cash began appearing in his mailbox. Omidyar didn't know it yet, but he had launched what would become one of the greatest successes in the history of American business. +

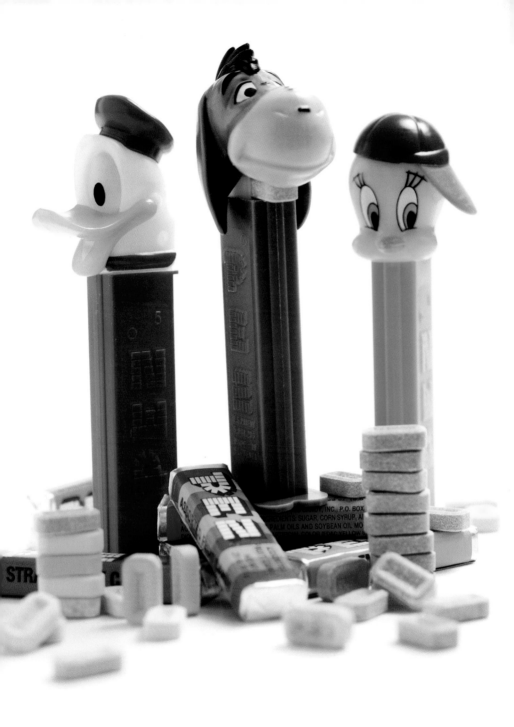

Part of Omidyar's inspiration to start an online auction Web site was his fiancée's desire to sell her PEZ dispenser collection.

In 1967, Pierre Omidyar was born in the bustling city of Paris, France.

NOT JUST ANOTHER KID

I f a good college education could have been attained in Iran in the early 1960s, Pierre Omidyar may never have been born. The lack of such educational opportunities motivated his grandparents to send their children to Paris, France, for college. Pierre's mother studied linguistics and his father went to medical school. During this time, they met, fell in love, and married. On June 21, 1967, their only child, Pierre, was born.

The young boy had little time to establish his roots in Paris. He learned to speak English at a bilingual school, which was fortunate, because when he was six, his family moved to Washington DC. His father started a new position as a doctor at Johns Hopkins University in nearby Baltimore, Maryland. It was while living in Washington DC that Pierre developed a fascination with computers.

His curiosity prompted him to sneak out of gym class in seventh grade and into a closet to study a computer his science teacher was storing there. While the other students were playing sports and games, he was busy teaching himself to program the computer. Such interest in electronics allowed him to gain great expertise at an early age.

Though his parents separated when he was young, both played a critical role in his upbringing. In a 2000 interview, Omidyar spoke about his father, who was particularly influential:

I lived with my mom, but my dad was always around. I remember when I was younger spending weekends with my dad, who is a surgeon and a medical doctor, doing rounds with him. We would spend maybe 45 minutes in the car going from one hospital to the next and we'd have some great conversations. That's one of my fond childhood memories.[1]

DR. ELAHÉ MIR-DJALALI OMIDYAR

Pierre's family instilled in him the value of an education. Not only was his father a doctor, but his mother earned her PhD at the Sorbonne, a highly acclaimed university in Paris. Dr. Elahé Mir-Djalali Omidyar forged a successful career of her own as a linguist, which is an expert in the science of language.

Dr. Mir-Djalali Omidyar taught linguistics at Georgetown University and the University of California at Berkeley. She also gained great expertise on subjects such as cross-cultural communication and Persian studies. Persia is the former name of Iran.

She remained closely bound to her Iranian heritage and founded a nonprofit organization based in Washington DC called the Roshan Cultural Heritage Institute. This organization works to help people understand and embrace the importance of their cultural past. It is particularly focused on helping those with Iranian backgrounds appreciate their culture.

Dr. Mir-Djalali Omidyar also worked as an executive at the Institute of Comparative Social and Cultural Studies, which promotes better understanding between people from different cultures.

TO HAWAII AND BACK

Pierre did not remain in one place long enough to make many friends his own age. After living in Washington DC for several years, he and his mother moved to Hawaii when he was a young teen. He completed grades eight and nine there.

Then he and his mom returned to Washington, where Pierre attended high school. He had grown close to other kids in Hawaii, which made leaving that state rather difficult. The experience of moving every few years made Pierre grow up quickly, though. So did spending a lot of time with adults because so few children were around. Pierre was clearly more mature than others his age.

Pierre's parents instilled in him several important beliefs. One was the belief that he was capable of achieving anything. Another belief was that one person can make a difference in the world. Finally, Pierre's parents instilled in him the value of connecting with others. He recalled spending time with his father:

RESISTING TEMPTATION

When Pierre worked on a computer program to set up class schedules in high school, he considered helping his own cause. He later admitted that he had thought about creating a favorable schedule for himself, but he did not act on it. He said, "I resisted the temptation to put in some code there to make sure I never had classes on Friday, because I wouldn't have been able to get away with it, but I thought about it."[2]

We'd spend time in the car talking about what was going on with [his patients], their stories. And what he communicated to me was the rich human component there. What was important about his

In the mid-1980s, Apple computers looked very different from the way they look today.

work was his connection with his patients, not just in the operating room but connecting with them as human beings.[3]

Upon returning to Washington DC, Pierre enrolled at St. Andrews Episcopal High School. He was not a good student, in his opinion, but he discovered his passion for computers and began maximizing his talents at an early age. In high school, he started programming an Apple II computer and began computerizing the card catalog at the school library for six dollars an hour. He also worked on the computer program that produced class schedules for the school.

A PASSION FOR COMPUTERS

There was no doubt about his emphasis of study in 1984 when Omidyar arrived at Tufts University, just a few miles from Boston, Massachusetts. Omidyar majored in computer science just as the world of computer technology was about to change the world forever. At Tufts, he learned more specifically what he was capable of achieving.

Omidyar decided to major in computer engineering, the study of computer hardware and software. He was accepted into the program at Tufts but quickly found the course work too difficult. He took a required chemistry class for which he had little interest. He studied diligently but performed poorly. He then transferred out of the computer engineering program and into the liberal arts program to study basic computer science.

His passion was programming Apple computers. At the time, Apple was revolutionizing the computer industry and helping

THE MAN BEHIND APPLE

The man who spearheaded the success of Apple computers was company cofounder Steve Jobs. In the late 1970s, he helped design and market a line of personal computers such as the Apple I, Apple II, and Macintosh.

Jobs later cofounded and served as chief executive officer (CEO) of Pixar Animation Studios, which has produced some of the most popular and critically acclaimed animated films of all time, including *Toy Story*, *A Bug's Life*, *Monsters, Inc.*, *Finding Nemo*, *The Incredibles*, *Cars*, and *Ratatouille*.

IMPROVING GRADES

Omidyar has referred to himself as "one of those guys that didn't really study" and so admits that he was not a good student.[4] He did, however, perform fairly well at Tufts University. He managed to improve his grades every semester and graduated with a commendable 3.01 grade point average (GPA). According to Omidyar, the fact that he ended up with a 3.01 GPA after four years of course work indicates how bad his early grades were.

bring computers into American homes. Rather than work on one of the many personal computers in the college computer lab, Omidyar taught himself programming on a Macintosh, an Apple computer, in his dorm room.

He not only became quite adept at it, but he enjoyed it enough to seek out an internship as a Macintosh programmer during the summer after his junior year. He scoured the classified ads in a magazine for Apple users called *Macworld* and sent out letters to companies that created Mac software. He earned a spot at Innovative Data Design in California, one of the first companies to create programs allowing Macintosh users to draw images with their computers. He was soon offered a full-time job, so he took off the fall semester to work. Then he returned to Tufts.

Omidyar's career was heading in the right direction. The self-professed geek was on his way to incredible business success. +

At Tufts University, Omidyar studied computer science.

In 1984, Silicon Valley was growing due to the boom
in the high-tech industry.

INTO THE REAL WORLD

When Omidyar walked into Innovative Data
Design for his internship in 1988, he fit
right in with the other programmers. He
sported a beard, ponytail, and aviator-type glasses.
He also liked to talk about not only computers but

also philosophy and whether UFOs (unidentified flying objects) and beings from outer space actually existed.

Innovative Data Design was located in Silicon Valley, an area just outside San Francisco. This area had become the center of the United States' growing technology industry. It received its nickname from a piece of electronic chips used as components in computers. Following his internship and job at Innovative Data Design, Omidyar spent one more semester at Tufts.

Omidyar then got a job at Claris, which developed software for Apple. Apple actually owned Claris, but intended to sell it so it could become an independent company. When that plan changed, many employees left Claris, including Omidyar.

Omidyar joined with a group of Claris coworkers to form the Ink Development Corporation in 1991. Their idea was to create software for pen-based computers, a technology that some believed would be the wave of the future. The idea was that instead of a keyboard and mouse, people would use a stylus, which is a writing utensil used on computer screens.

The public, however, simply did not embrace the notion. Omidyar and the Ink Development

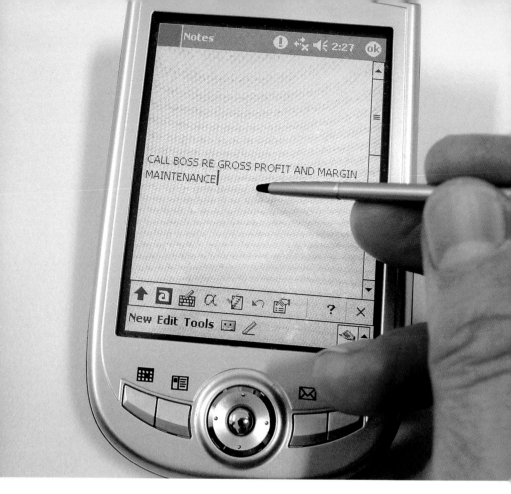

Pen-based computer technology was later used in the PalmPilot and other personal desk assistants.

Corporation were forced to look elsewhere for success. Fortunately, the company had also begun creating software for online shopping businesses. Since the name of their company no longer fit, they changed it to eShop. Omidyar's partners, however, were reluctant to place the new business on the Internet. They simply did not fully grasp the possibilities of the Internet as a selling tool.

Omidyar, however, saw great potential in the Internet, so in 1994 he left eShop to head out on his own.

Omidyar maintained his stock in eShop, which turned out to be a very profitable move. The purchasing of stock allows the buyer to own a piece of a business and gain financially when the business earns money. But buying stock is also a risk because one can lose money when the business fares poorly. Omidyar, however earned more than $1 million two years later when technology giant Microsoft bought out eShop.

In the meantime, Omidyar had fulfilled his desire to work with the Internet. In December 1994, he became a software engineer with General Magic, a new mobile communications company that sought to build computers that could work with telephones and fax machines. He worked there until July 1996, almost one year after starting AuctionWeb. By then,

THE PALMPILOT PEN

Omidyar's Ink Development Corporation and other businesses failed to create a market for pen-based computers, but a company called Palm Inc. did find success several years later with the PalmPilot.

It features a stylus pen and a handheld personal computer. The PalmPilot was first sold in 1996. Palm later developed and marketed some of the first smartphones: cell phones that allow users to communicate via e-mail, connect to the Internet, and do many other things.

A VIEW OF THE WORLD

Omidyar has been described as a libertarian, which is someone who believes in the right to freedom of thought and action unrestricted by the government. That philosophy helped drive him to create AuctionWeb. He is proud that the site has provided people great freedom of action in both buying and selling.

AuctionWeb was bringing in more money than he was being paid at General Magic.

Omidyar could have retired with his million-dollar payout from Microsoft. But instead, he left General Magic behind and threw his efforts into AuctionWeb.

Deciding to work full-time on the Web site was not easy for Omidyar. He asked himself, "You get a million dollars? When you're 29? Hey, take some time off. Take a *lot* of time off."[1] Omidyar had never been driven by financial wealth, though. He drew great satisfaction from providing a service to thousands of users.

His belief that people are generally good-hearted was put to the test. Buyers and sellers had to trust each other for his site to work. He advised those using AuctionWeb to treat others the way they wanted to be treated. He was rewarded when sellers, who trusted buyers to pay for purchased items, shipped the items before the money was received.

One major attraction for users was the selling process itself. Sellers were able to entice buyers by displaying items on the site and promoting them through their own written advertisements. Some sellers set a price for an item that would then be sold to anyone willing to pay that amount.

Others put items up for bid with a time limit, which allowed them to receive the maximum amount of money the market would bear. Potential buyers continued to place bids on the items for sale, which would then be awarded to the highest bidder when the time limit for bidding had elapsed.

The convenience of the selling and bidding process for both sellers and buyers proved to be arguably the greatest attraction for AuctionWeb, which was later called eBay. It allowed sellers to make money without paying for outside advertising and forcing them to lure buyers to their places of business. It allowed buyers to shop without leaving their homes and made it easy to comparison shop for the best price on a product.

THE FEEDBACK FORUM

Buyers and sellers did have disagreements on occasion, and they usually e-mailed Omidyar directly to mediate their disputes. In the early days of AuctionWeb, he received approximately one dozen e-mails a day from users complaining about one another. He certainly did not want to be responsible for settling users' disagreements. So in responding to each complaint, he let both parties know that they had to work it out for themselves.

In February 1996, he announced the launch of the Feedback Forum, which offered users an opportunity to express both negative and positive feelings about the site and make suggestions for improvements. Omidyar explained the benefits of the Feedback Forum in a letter on his site,

Most people are honest. And they

UNCLE GRIFF

An intriguing character gained notoriety as AuctionWeb gained users. He was a bearded man named Jim Griffith who had spent 20 difficult years in New York City, first struggling as an actor and then as a decorative artist. By the time the site had been launched, the middle-aged Griffith had moved to Vermont to carve out a new life.

Soon, he found AuctionWeb. He grew addicted to the site and began spending time on its Bulletin Board. He began giving advice to others about computers and AuctionWeb under the nickname of Uncle Griff. His guidance was often accompanied by silliness; he once claimed to be wearing a flowered dress after having just milked the cows!

When an earlier problem with depression returned, Griffith stopped contributing. He received a call from the AuctionWeb business manager Jeff Skoll asking why. Griffith was gratified to learn that users had been asking about him. Skoll then hired him at a salary of $100 a month as AuctionWeb's first official customer-support person. He still works with the site as its dean of education. He speaks at seminars, hosts a radio program, gives advice on how to buy and sell on eBay, and wrote a book titled *The Official eBay Bible*.

mean well. . . . But some people are dishonest. Or deceptive. This is true here, in the newsgroups, in the classifieds, and right next door. It's a fact of life. But here, those people can't hide. We'll drive them away. Protect others from them. This grand hope depends on your active participation. Become a registered user. Use our feedback forum. Give praise where it is due; make complaints where appropriate. . . .

Remember that you are usually dealing with individuals, just like yourself. Subject to making mistakes. Well-meaning, but wrong on occasion. That's just human. We can live with that. We can deal with that. We can still make deals with that.[2]

The Feedback Forum allows users to give one another a rating of plus one, neutral, or negative one. A computer program is used to tabulate the scores, and a seller whose score reaches negative four is banned from the site. The Feedback Forum has become a vital monitoring device on the site, allowing users to write about their experiences with particular buyers and sellers. That, in turn, gives other users important information about which buyers and sellers can or cannot be trusted in the business transaction process.

Omidyar was not finished making changes to AuctionWeb. He soon added the Bulletin Board, which allows users who are familiar with the site to give others suggestions on how to buy, sell, bid, and ship. That, too, was a rousing success.

AuctionWeb's success translated into profits. In April 1996, the site earned $2,500. That figure doubled in May and again in June, when revenues reached $10,000.

Omidyar knew that for AuctionWeb to keep growing, he needed a business plan, which is a statement of business goals, ways they can be achieved, and reasons supporting why a business could become successful. He brought in Jeff Skoll, a Canadian friend with an MBA from Stanford, to develop the plan. It would become more apparent with every day and every dollar that, to Omidyar, money was merely a tool to improve the lives of others. +

Omidyar never imagined his auction Web site would become
so successful in such a short time.

Omidyar's old friend, Jeff Skoll, joined AuctionWeb in 1996.

NEW TALENT AND NEW INVESTORS

O midyar enjoyed running AuctionWeb. He was thrilled that his dream of helping others help themselves had become a reality. He was also thrilled when the profits from the site began to rise in 1996.

The problem was that he knew little about business. So he decided to hire someone who did. He immediately thought of Jeff Skoll, whom he had met through friends several years earlier. Skoll had earned a perfect 4.0 GPA while completing an electrical engineering degree at the University of Toronto. After graduating, the native Canadian founded two high-tech companies of his own: Skoll Engineering and Micros on the Move Ltd. And he had just completed an MBA degree from the Stanford School of Business.

Like Omidyar, Skoll saw the Internet as the wave of the future, and he was restless. He landed a job as an Internet specialist with Knight-Ridder—a company that owned a string of newspapers. In the fall of 1995, Skoll turned down a job offer from Omidyar, believing that a Web site that allowed people to buy and sell items was doomed to failure. Like Omidyar's former eShop colleagues, Skoll underestimated the potential of the Internet as a selling tool.

A year later, Skoll changed his mind. He began to understand the power of the Internet as a tool for commerce. He even came to realize that the Internet was a financial threat to newspapers, which depended on classified ads for much of their income. After all, sellers on the Internet could use as much space as was needed to advertise their goods and could also post pictures of their items. AuctionWeb even allowed buyers and sellers to communicate online. Skoll quit his job at Knight-Ridder and came to work full-time for AuctionWeb in 1996.

Skoll's talent and mindset proved to be the perfect counterbalance to Omidyar's. As Omidyar explained, "I tended to think more intuitively, and he could say, 'Okay, let's see how we can actually get that done.'"[1]

MARY LOU SONG

Omidyar wanted to build a company that was embraced all over the world. He also wanted to bring cultural diversity to his own business. The man with French and Iranian roots had already brought aboard Skoll, a Jewish Canadian. He soon recruited a 27-year-old Korean-American woman named Mary Lou Song.

Song had an undergraduate degree in journalism from Northwestern University and a graduate degree in communications from Stanford University. She had worked for a short time as a reporter at small newspapers in Michigan before landing a job in public relations in California. She spoke with Skoll at a party, and he informed her that AuctionWeb needed someone to run its public relations. She visited the AuctionWeb offices and came away quite unimpressed. After all, the offices were cramped and disorganized. She also spoke with Omidyar and was surprised to learn that he was more interested in helping people than in making money.

She then examined the site, which at the time looked quite dull. Even so, she found the offer to work there intriguing enough to take the job as public relations manager.

TARGETING INVESTORS

Skoll worked tirelessly. He was originally intrigued with the idea of selling auction management software to other Internet sites, but the enormous growth of AuctionWeb made that unnecessary. Skoll and Omidyar then set their sights on attracting financial backing from venture capitalists—people or groups who invest in companies with the goal of receiving a share of future profits. They sought investors who could sink money into eBay, the company that owned AuctionWeb.

In early 1997, Mark Del Vecchio, the general manager of electronic publishing for the *Hartford Courant*, expressed his concern to his superiors that AuctionWeb was taking away classified ad business from the newspaper. A lot was at stake—the newspaper industry received approximately 40 percent of its income from classified ads. Del Vecchio sought to convince Times Mirror, the company that owned the *Hartford Courant* and many of the largest newspapers in the country, to purchase AuctionWeb.

Del Vecchio decided to set up a meeting. He e-mailed Skoll three times but received no reply. Finally he decided to go to the AuctionWeb offices with colleague Jim Schwartz, but there was no

AN ELEVATOR JOKE

Until 1997, the AuctionWeb office was quite disorganized. Nobody was even responsible for ordering and purchasing supplies. Omidyar and Skoll finally realized they needed an office manager, and Sandra Gaeta was hired.

A few weeks before she started work, Gaeta joined her future colleagues at a holiday party lunch at a nearby restaurant. All five employees stepped on an elevator, which led to some dark humor. They laughed when someone suggested that if anything terrible happened to the elevator, that would be the end of AuctionWeb.

receptionist to greet them upon their arrival. They began speaking with Skoll, who was working in his office. Then Omidyar walked in holding a plastic bag full of computer parts. He explained they were needed to build a new server to keep the site running.

The two stunned visitors noticed overstuffed canvas bags throughout the office. Omidyar explained that they were filled with envelopes containing AuctionWeb user fees that had yet to be opened. Schwartz privately marveled at the idea of a business that was receiving checks that could not be opened fast enough. He believed AuctionWeb had potential. He spoke to Omidyar and Skoll about Times Mirror purchasing some of the site, but recommended to his own company that it should buy all of the site.

Soon after, Skoll and Omidyar flew to New York to meet with

The Times Mirror Company, now owned by Tribune Company, is headquartered in Los Angeles, California.

Times Mirror executives. They expressed an openness to sell the entire site for the right price. Skoll believed that the success of AuctionWeb, which still suffered from archaic technology and poor organization, could end quickly. Omidyar was also considering taking his professional life in a different direction. But they could not convince Times Mirror of the long-term potential of online auctioning. Times Mirror had the opportunity to purchase AuctionWeb for $40 million, but it declined the offer.

THE BEST MOVE NEVER MADE

That decision proved to be a huge mistake for Times Mirror and quite fortunate for Omidyar and Skoll. In March 2000, the Tribune Company purchased Times Mirror for $8 billion. By that time, Omidyar's site was worth more than twice that amount.

In 1997, Omidyar approached former eShop colleague Bruce Dunlevie, who was a partner in an investment company called Benchmark Capital. Dunlevie was not especially interested, but he convinced Benchmark copartner Bob Kagle to join in as Omidyar gave a presentation about the benefits of investing in AuctionWeb.

The meeting was a disaster from the start. Omidyar arrived with nothing to present—not even a slide show about his company. And he explained that with Skoll out of town, he could give

Benchmark few financial details about the potential investment. Then, when Omidyar attempted to give Dunlevie and Kagle a tour of the AuctionWeb site, he discovered that it was temporarily down.

Though the Benchmark executives remained friendly, they were not about to invest $5 million at that time. The meeting broke up, but Kagle was intrigued enough to visit the site on his own later in the day. Impressed by what he saw, he bid on a fishing decoy. He was even more impressed when he was outbid, because it showed the potential of the site to attract top dollar for items sold.

As time passed, Kagle grew more excited about the notion of bringing individual sellers and consumers from around the world together in a single Internet spot. He was not yet prepared to invest, but he spoke with Skoll about the future of the site. In June 1997,

EBAY CAFÉ

A persistent argument over the purpose of the AuctionWeb Bulletin Board led Omidyar to make a change in late 1996. He divided the Bulletin Board into two separate boards on the site. One was renamed the Q & A Board, which served to answer any questions users might have. The second was called eBay Café, which allowed users to socialize with one another. The name eBay Café was chosen from among 20 possibilities in a vote by users. It beat out other suggestions including Backyard Fence and Kitchen Sink.

when AuctionWeb began growing faster than ever, Benchmark paid $5 million for 21.5 percent of the company. Despite the impressive growth of the site, neither Kagle nor Dunlevie could have predicted that such a comparatively small investment would eventually make them $4 billion. Their investment resulted in one of the biggest payoffs in the history of business. +

In 1998, Benchmark Capital's partners included, *from left to right*, Bruce Dunlevie, Kevin Harvey, Andrew Rachleff, Bob Kagle, and David Beirne.

Collectors of all ages used AuctionWeb to buy retired Beanie Babies.

THE GREAT EBAY FLOOD

In early 1997, the explosion in popularity of AuctionWeb made the boom of 1996 pale in comparison. The 1997 boom was driven greatly by the cuddly stuffed animals known as Beanie Babies, which were made by toy manufacturer

Ty Warner. There were nine kinds of Beanie Babies, with such colorful names as Flash the dolphin and Pinchers the lobster. Ty Warner shrewdly took some Beanie Babies off the market and began manufacturing new ones. Every time one of the plush toys was retired, collectors launched a search to find them.

It proved to be an ideal situation for AuctionWeb, which was flooded with Beanie Baby swapping. In April 1997, more than 2,500 Beanie Babies were listed on the site. In fact, listings for the plush toys had increased so rapidly, they were given their own category on AuctionWeb. Beanie Babies that had been sold in stores for $5 were receiving average bids of $33. In May alone, $500,000 worth of Beanie Babies was sold on the site. Beanie Babies made up 6.6 percent of all the items listed on AuctionWeb.

Those stuffed animals were just one type of collectible that was popular on AuctionWeb. In late 1996, all of the fastest-growing categories of items on the site were collectibles. Popular categories

BIG MONEY ITEMS

In early 1997, AuctionWeb was not just hosting a greater volume of bidding—the items were also gaining in value and notoriety. Among items being auctioned in February were a check signed by famed 1950s actress Marilyn Monroe that sold for nearly $1,995 and a 1959 Barbie doll that went for $7,999, a new record for the site.

A 1959 Barbie doll was one of the items that brought
high bids to an early auction on AuctionWeb.

included coins, stamps, baseball cards, and other
vintage toys and games. AuctionWeb provided the
perfect outlet for anyone buying or selling these
collectibles.

Rare items most often could not be found at
stores within driving range of those who sought
them. In addition, people did not even know where
to track them down. But on AuctionWeb, buyers

could easily find whatever they wanted. In one four-and-a-half-month period in late 1996, listings of antiques and collectibles increased 350 percent.

The key was word of mouth. Coin collectors told other coin collectors about AuctionWeb. Other kinds of collectors soon did the same. By early 1997, the site was no longer dominated by buyers seeking computer-related items. Almost 80 percent of the listings were for antiques and collectibles.

SOARING TO NEW HEIGHTS

The popularity of AuctionWeb was growing by leaps and bounds, as was Internet use in general. In the spring of 1996, the number of Americans and Canadians using the Internet was estimated at fewer than 19 million. That total had zoomed to 50 million by December. New advances had been made in creating and distributing Web pages on the Internet, which meant that suddenly anyone could put material up and distribute it over the Web.

A GENEROUS COMMUNITY

When one eBay Café poster revealed that she did not own a computer and could only use the site from work, it spurred a group of other users into action. They all chipped in, donating computer parts that they then had assembled. Soon they shipped an entire computer to the woman, who could then post on nights and weekends.

What became known as the Great eBay Flood had begun. The fact that so many new people were using the World Wide Web—and Omidyar's site specifically—brought both good and bad news. The good news was that the site was helping more buyers and sellers than ever before. The bad news was that its server kept crashing from the increased traffic. Users became frustrated when quite often they lost AuctionWeb just as they were bidding or posting new items for sale. It also took new listings an entire day to appear on the site. The problem became so acute that users were advised on the site not to visit AuctionWeb during the peak evening hours of 5:00 to 9:00 p.m. in Pacific Standard Time.

Omidyar and Skoll decided to take drastic steps. First they attempted to discourage frequent AuctionWeb users from visiting the site, but those users refused to slow down. Then Omidyar and Skoll created a credit approval process in an attempt to drive away sellers who had proven to be unreliable in paying their user fees. That move had the opposite effect of what was intended. The nine staff members were overwhelmed with paperwork. And to top it off, the office computer crashed and destroyed several days of billing records. The staff was, to say the least, becoming discouraged.

The growing engineering department, headed by new hire Mike Wilson, eventually gained control of the problem. And despite the issues with the site, profits continued to soar. AuctionWeb earned approximately $350,000 in 1996, and projections indicated that figure would rise to $4.3 million the following year. Such success could be hidden no longer. Competitor sites, such as Auction Block, AuctionNet, and Auction Universe, sprang up on the Internet, but they proved far less popular than AuctionWeb.

OMIDYAR'S ADVICE

Omidyar has said that he enjoys talking to young people because he believes they are passionate and have great ideas. Many of them say that they too would like to start a business from scratch. What is his reply? Omidyar said in a 2000 interview,

Well if they say, "I want to do exactly what you did and compete with eBay," I say, "Don't bother. Don't quit your day job." That's pretty rare. . . . And, what I tell them is a number of things.

I say that you should pursue your passion. If you're passionate about something and you work hard, then I think you'll be successful. If you start a business because you think you're going to make a lot of money at it, then you probably won't be successful, because that's the wrong reason to start a business. You have to really believe in what you're doing, be passionate about it so that you will put in the hours and the hard work that it takes to actually succeed there, and then you'll be successful. . . .

And don't let people who you may respect and who you believe know what they're talking about, don't let them tell you it can't be done, because often they will tell you it can't be done, and it's just because they don't have the courage to try.[1]

TAKING ON A CHALLENGE

A site called Onsale, however, did provide some spirited competition. In mid-1997, Skoll was asked by an Onsale representative whether AuctionWeb would be interested in selling its customer list. The request was turned down flatly, but soon AuctionWeb's engineers detected devices called bots on the site. Bots are computer programs that are used to perform specific functions, such as gathering information about a Web site's users. The bots were discovered to have been placed on the AuctionWeb site by Onsale. When confronted, Onsale executives claimed they did not know about the actions of their employees.

THE FALL VISION TOUR

Omidyar, Skoll, and Song set out in November 1997 to bring attention to the Web site now officially known as eBay. Working with a public relations firm, they launched a promotional campaign

FROM AUCTIONWEB TO EBAY

In mid-1997, Omidyar and Skoll decided to change the name of their site from AuctionWeb to eBay. They decided to make the change because most users, as well as the media, referred to the site as eBay. The new name came from Omidyar's original company name, for which the Web address had always been ebay.com. In September 1997, a new design of the site was launched, which included the colorful eBay logo that is now well recognized.

called the Fall Vision Tour. Omidyar was interviewed by journalists and industry analysts on the East and West Coasts. He was prepared to answer some tough questions about the company, but to his dismay, journalists asked very few questions. They did not know what to ask because the notion of online auctioning was so foreign to them.

He came prepared with slides and charts showing the rapid growth of eBay. He also explained that users were told to report incidents of fraud to the National Fraud Information Center or the US Postal Service and to copy eBay on the report so fraudulent users could be suspended from using the site. When further questioned about fraud, Omidyar responded by stating that from among the 1 million auctions during a recent month, only 30 complaints had been lodged.

The Fall Vision Tour, however, was mostly disappointing. Many of the journalists showed little or no interest in eBay, and one of the

ON STRIKING IT RICH

Omidyar has used his earnings to help others. He believes doing so is one way he can express his thanks to the people who made eBay successful. "It happened so fast, and on such a large scale, that it was actually overwhelming," he stated in a 2004 interview. "[My wife] Pam and I, our reaction was that it was a sense of responsibility to put it to good use. I didn't feel like, boy, I'm entitled to this fortune because of all the work I did. eBay's success is based on the eBay community's success."[2]

television networks abruptly canceled its interview
with Omidyar.

Song had run into the same problem in trying
to generate media interest in eBay, so she decided
to take a different angle. She told reporters that
Omidyar launched eBay as a way to help his fiancée
sell her collection of PEZ dispensers. The idea that a
man would create a Web site to help his fiancée sell
her collectibles finally drew interest from the media.
The story was in the local newspaper the next day.

Being in the spotlight, however, did not suit
Omidyar. His passion for eBay revolved around the
tight-knit community formed by the site's users and
his colleagues. He wished to remain involved with
eBay, but it was time for him to hand over the reins
to someone else. +

Under Omidyar's direction, eBay had become
very successful by the end of 1997.

In 1998, eBay opened its doors to new CEO Meg Whitman.

A NEW CEO AND PHILANTHROPY

The world of eBay changed dramatically in late 1997 when Omidyar and Skoll decided to sell its stock to the public. The announcement would be launched by an Initial Public Offering (IPO), during which stock in a company is made available to anyone who is interested in purchasing it.

The two partners agreed that completing such a complex and important business move successfully was beyond their levels of expertise. So they agreed to bring in an experienced person to replace Omidyar as the CEO of eBay. They set their sights on Meg Whitman.

Whitman had built an impressive career since earning business degrees from Princeton and Harvard in the late 1970s. Most recently, she had developed a sterling reputation as general manager of the preschool division of Hasbro, one of the premier toy-manufacturing corporations in the world. She had been greatly responsible for managing and marketing such successful toy brands as Playskool. She also was responsible for introducing the Teletubbies to the United States

FINALLY TAKING THE PLUNGE

The Times Mirror Corporation regretted not investing in eBay when it had had the chance in 1997. After all, eBay had enjoyed a tremendous rise in profits after Times Mirror turned down an opportunity to purchase all or part of the company. Times Mirror didn't want to make the same mistake twice. Later that year, the company bought online auction business Auction Universe, which ultimately failed to compete with eBay. In 1998, Times Mirror sold Auction Universe to Classified Ventures, a group of newspapers that hoped to use the site to sell more classified advertising.

and for relaunching the popular vintage toy Mr. Potato Head.

It was not going to be easy convincing Whitman to come aboard. She was perfectly content at Hasbro, which was based in Rhode Island, and her neurosurgeon husband worked conveniently close by at Massachusetts General Hospital in Boston. When first offered the job with eBay in the fall of 1997, she turned it down. She was called again three weeks later, this time agreeing to visit. The night before her flight to California, she looked at the Web site and found it shockingly dull. She felt that the next day's interview would be a waste of her time and considered canceling it.

EYE-OPENING EXPERIENCE

At the interview, Whitman met with Omidyar, Skoll, and Benchmark executive Bob Kagle. She came away impressed with the eBay philosophy of helping people conduct business who did not have the means to do it on their own. She agreed to meet again at the eBay offices on the day before Thanksgiving. She realized that a company with virtually no expenses, such as shipping, packing, or storage, could prove extremely profitable.

Omidyar and Whitman knew the potential of eBay,
especially in the collectibles market.

Whitman returned home and told her husband
that she had "stumbled onto something that had
unbelievable potential."[1] Omidyar offered her the
job in late December, but she took some time to
decide. In May 1998, she accepted the position.

She officially became CEO, and Omidyar stayed on as chairman of the board. In September of that year, both were rewarded when the IPO sold more than $2 billion in eBay stock.

Omidyar had always believed that wealth was merely a tool to help others. It felt strange to him and wife Pam to be so tremendously rich. Their stock in eBay was worth $6.6 billion by the end of 1998. They did not live a wealthy lifestyle, though. Omidyar owned just four suits— and he had purchased them all to help promote the company in the Fall Vision Tour. The couple drove a Volkswagen car and decorated their home

EMBRACING ELVIS

Though iconic early rock-and-roll singer Elvis Presley has been dead for more than 30 years, he still has millions of passionate fans. In August 1998, as 50,000 of those fans made their way to Memphis, Tennessee, for Elvis Week, eBay decided to join the celebration.

That weekend eBay launched its first Elvis memorabilia site, which was inspired by employee Robin Rosaaen. In her early 50s at the time, Rosaaen was an Elvis fanatic who had seen him perform 72 times before his death in August 1977. Over many years, Rosaaen built a large private collection of Elvis memorabilia. She even wrote a book titled *All the King's Things: The Ultimate Elvis Memorabilia Book*. After landing a job in eBay's billing department, she gave Omidyar a copy of the book and discussed starting an Elvis auction category on the site. Seeing the potential in this idea, Omidyar agreed.

The rest is history. The Elvis category was highly successful. The number of Elvis collectibles quickly increased from 150 to more than 2,000. One Tennessee woman sold a four-minute, black-and-white movie of Elvis leaving a Florida hotel for $12,500.

with budget brands from the local department store. They even planned a move to an area outside of Las Vegas, Nevada, because they believed those living in their Silicon Valley neighborhood had become too obsessed with money.

Their philanthropic journey began when they discussed and debated appropriate targets for their money. They concluded that more traditional charitable efforts rarely solved problems in society. Like many grant givers, they hoped for some accountability, or evidence of what had been achieved. Also, the sheer number of charitable possibilities overwhelmed Omidyar. "There were too many good causes," he said. "How do you do it well?"[2]

CHOOSING CHARITIES

The couple sought to make charitable contributions that

WEEKEND GETAWAY

In October 1998, the entire eBay staff of more than 40 people rode two buses to Asilomar, a resort on the coast of the Pacific Ocean. The trip was intended to give employees the chance to celebrate the success of the company's recent IPO. The two primary events of the weekend were the eBay Olympics and the eBay Fashion Show. Employees challenged each other in relay races and a tug-of-war as part of the eBay Olympics. But the fashion show proved more memorable. Skoll and several other men showed off on stage wearing dresses and high heels, while Whitman paraded around in an outfit that resembled a man's suit.

GETTING RICHER

In July 1999, *Forbes* magazine identified Omidyar as the thirty-sixth-wealthiest individual in the United States, with a total worth of $10.1 billion. He had achieved this wealth just nine months after eBay's IPO, when it had begun selling stock to the public. Skoll was eightieth on the *Forbes* list with $4.8 billion. And while Whitman did not make the list, she was worth more than $1 billion, despite having just joined eBay. Approximately 75 eBay staff members had earned multiple millions of dollars since the IPO, and even its newest employees had made hundreds of thousands of dollars.

would help people help themselves. Following the IPO in September of 1998, he and wife Pam established the Omidyar Foundation, which provides money for nonprofit organizations. One that received Omidyar funds was KaBOOM!, an organization that creates play spaces for children across the United States. Another was New Profit Inc., which provides funding and other support to groups involved in causes such as early reading programs and public health clinics.

The Omidyars looked to help find solutions to problems rather than provide money for temporary help. Rather than giving funds directly to feed hungry children, for instance, they worked toward creating jobs for parents of hungry children. The parents could then afford to feed their own children.

In 2000, the Omidyars donated $10 million to their

Jumpstart, a reading intervention program,
was one investment of New Profit Inc.

alma mater, Tufts University. But they made certain
the money would be utilized for specific programs,
not rolled into the university's general endowment
fund. For instance, some of the money was used to
provide scholarships for students who had worked
in community-development projects, and some of it
was used to fund students who agreed to volunteer
their time and efforts working in poor Boston
neighborhoods.

The Omidyars had always been imbued with
the spirit of charity, but they now had the money

and means to make a difference. Other young wealthy people felt they also needed to give back. In November 1998, the Omidyars and 40 other couples, none of whom who were over 35 years old, met at the home of Yahoo! founder Jerry Yang to discuss possible philanthropic efforts. The total net worth of those in attendance was about $30 billion. Omidyar's philanthropic journey was just beginning. While he continued to help eBay flourish, he also set his sights on making the world a better place to live. +

The Omidyar Foundation contributed to KaBOOM!, an organization that builds playgrounds for children.

The eBay company continued to grow throughout 1998.

PROSPERITY, GIVING, AND A SETBACK

Nine months after Whitman announced her resignation from Hasbro to join eBay, she received a phone call from her old boss. The head of Hasbro had not been able to understand why Whitman had wanted to take a job at an unknown company on the other side of the country. But after the eBay IPO, he told Whitman that now he knew exactly why she had taken the job.

Other major online corporations had lost their financial momentum by buying up smaller companies in moves that failed. But eBay's momentum did not slow down. The company opened new auction categories and trading formats. Whitman remained committed to the still-thriving collector business. Listings for collector coins, which were among the first items on the original AuctionWeb, had doubled in the past year.

One reason for further optimism was that eBay had gone global. Its first stop was Germany, where the Alando auction site had great success. In early 1999, the auction site had been started by six young Germans: the three Samwer brothers and three of their friends. One of the brothers had researched eBay during a visit to Silicon Valley and came away impressed. Upon his return home, he and his associates developed an auction

GREAT COLLECTIONS

One idea that did not work well for eBay was the creation of a category called Great Collections, launched in October 1999. In this category, expensive artwork, antiques, and collectibles were to be sold. The idea was to raise the average selling price of items on the site, but not enough upscale buyers participated to make it worthwhile. The fear of fraud and delays in shipping items discouraged buyers.

In 1999, eBay acquired the German auction site
Alando and renamed it eBay.de.

site that focused on its user community. Their tiny
office with cheap furniture looked like the one
Omidyar and Skoll resided in during the early days
of AuctionWeb.

Starting in March 1999, Alando was off and
running in Germany, with more than 250,000 items
listed and approximately 50,000 users. Omidyar
flew to the capital city of Berlin to investigate. The
Samwer brothers were nervous to meet Omidyar,
whom they knew was a billionaire. To their surprise,
he arrived in a beat-up Volkswagen Golf rather than

a limousine. Omidyar saw potential in their site
and purchased Alando in late June for more than
$42 million in eBay stock. The site was then
renamed eBay.de. By the fall of 2000, more than
500,000 items were listed on eBay.de.

MORE ACQUISITIONS

Omidyar then set his sights on Great Britain,
deciding to build a new site rather than acquire
an existing one. After several delays, the site was
launched on July 4, 1999. Success was slow in
coming, though, because Internet use in general was
behind in Britain compared to in the United States.
The chief reason was that Internet users had to pay
the phone company for every minute online. Even
so, within a year, the British eBay site had overcome
its main competitor.

In 2001, eBay acquired another European
online site—this one based in Paris and called iBazar.
It boasted 2.4 million registered users and was the
top site in France, Italy, Spain, Belgium, Portugal,
and the Netherlands. By the fall of that year, eBay
and its affiliates were the leading online auction sites
in 16 of the 17 markets in which it competed. The
only exception was Japan, where eBay had launched

a site in late 1999. Competing auction site Yahoo! had entered the Japanese market five months earlier than eBay and quickly gained almost total dominance. But eBay found success in other Pacific markets, including Australia and South Korea.

THE EBAY FOUNDATION

While eBay was acquiring new companies, it was also focused on giving back to society. In 1998 the eBay Foundation was formed for the purpose of supporting local communities both economically and socially. Employee Karin Stahl was named head of the charitable

SCARY COMPETITION

During a ski vacation in Colorado in 1999, Whitman learned a piece of news that ruined her vacation: Internet giant Amazon was starting its own online auction site. She returned to the office to discover that eBay investors and directors, as well as stock market analysts, had been calling to ask whether the competition would be a problem. She told them everything was fine, but she was more than a bit nervous.

There were good reasons for her uneasiness. Amazon had online selling experience. Its online auction site also looked appealing. Whitman and her colleagues engaged in an intensive review of the competitor's site, and the more they learned about it, the less fearful they felt. They noted, for example, that nearly all the sellers on Amazon were big businesses, rather than the typical individuals and small businesses that posted on eBay. In addition, Amazon did not have message boards. It did not provide the tight-knit community that made eBay special.

The most prolific stamp collector on eBay tested both sites. He placed 50 identical stamps on Amazon and eBay. Just eight sold on Amazon, and 37 sold on eBay. As it turned out, Whitman had nothing to worry about.

funding organization. Stahl had been hired in October 1997 to head up the company's Powersellers program, and she had traveled to Guatemala to do charity work just before starting at eBay.

During that visit, Stahl had found that most of the people lived in tiny shacks without electricity or running water. Some were hungry and there was no medical care. Upon leaving Guatemala, Stahl promised several teachers in a local school that she would find a way to help the people and return. She believed she could improve the people's standard of living by helping them sell their native crafts on eBay.

Stahl kept that promise by returning regularly to Guatemala. In August 1998, she came bearing computers and printers donated by eBay. She and a group of volunteers set up the equipment in a school classroom. The next summer Stahl

EBAY MOTORS

In April 2000, eBay entered a new marketplace when it launched eBay Motors online. The new site did not sit well, however, with a motorcycle memorabilia fanatic named Scott Wellhausen. He did not know whether to post his wares on the main eBay site or on eBay Motors. He became so enraged that he created a Web site called Bikers Against Motors (BAM) in protest. He also posted a number of complaints on an eBay discussion board. Wellhausen and others began a boycott of eBay Motors, but the site succeeded.

FURBY FANATICS

A battery-operated talking stuffed animal toy called the Furby was all the rage on eBay during the 1998 holiday season. Furbies could be taught to speak a few phrases in English. Parents who wished to procure a Furby rushed onto eBay. The site sold 20,000 Furbies that season.

and her group returned with more computers, including 15 laptops donated by eBay. During another trip, an e-mail server was installed.

Stahl then tested the market with craft items she bought from the villagers, such as beaded jewelry, paintings, and various crafts. She listed the items on eBay, explaining in her postings that the money earned would support a school in Guatemala. In most cases, the crafts sold for more than Stahl had paid for them. In the end, Stahl believed that not only would the local craftspeople earn much more money, but they would learn how to function as businesspeople in the world economy.

A MAJOR CRASH

Despite having better technology than during its AuctionWeb days, in 1999 eBay still occasionally crashed for several hours at a time. So when the site went down just before 7:00 p.m. on June 10, nobody was worried.

This time, however, the site was not coming back up. The outage did not end until 22 hours later, and the site crashed a few times in the next few days as well. During that time, rival sites such as Yahoo! Auctions and Auction Universe saw significant jumps in usage. The outage caused eBay to lose considerable revenue and swayed the confidence of some stockholders who sold their eBay stock. Whitman feared that the outage would cause eBay to lose customers permanently. However, much to her relief, loyal eBay users were back within days.

Omidyar reflected on the outage in an interview the following year:

> *After a massive outage like that, you really anger your community. . . . A lot of them [were] dependent on us at that time for their livelihood and*

AN EXPLOSIVE DECISION

In February 1999, eBay banned the sale of guns and ammunition on the site. The company explained that it had become too difficult to ensure that buyers were legally able to purchase guns. The company also stressed that banning the sales of these items seemed the right thing to do.

The public response to eBay's decision was immediate and sharp. Public relations director Mary Lou Song received between 400 and 500 e-mails, some protesting and some applauding the move. All were upset, however, that eBay had not involved the community in making its decision.

still [are] today—so it's really a hardship. Even after that, they come back and they say, "Okay, well, we know you're doing your best. We're with you." And so I've always had, you know—I've always had kind of this unshakable faith that [eBay is] going to endure.[1]

Despite the setbacks resulting from the crash, eBay had become an international business and had spread its philanthropy outside of the United States by the end of the twentieth century. The vision of Omidyar had been realized. The founder of eBay could now use his wealth and vision to look for new challenges and become involved in new opportunities. +

Teachers and students in San Pedro, Guatemala, received
laptop computers from the eBay Foundation.

Part of what makes eBay successful is its ease of use
for both sellers and buyers.

THE EBAY LEGACY

The eBay site worked for many reasons, including the desire of millions of Americans to participate in the selling and purchasing of items online. But the one overriding factor that allowed it to succeed justified Omidyar's faith in his fellow human beings. And that factor was that people trusted one another well enough to do business while being hundreds or even thousands of miles apart.

The concept of an online auction and shopping site would never have succeeded if the transactions between buyers and sellers weren't being performed fairly. Omidyar and his colleagues at AuctionWeb, and later eBay, provided safeguards against dishonest buyers and sellers on the site. They proved that such a system could work, which in turn helped set off an online shopping boom in the United States, the extent of which few had thought possible just a few years earlier.

CONVENIENT SHOPPING

What Omidyar's site has provided arguably more than anything else is convenience for both sellers and buyers. Sellers must feature attractive descriptions and photos of their wares. They aren't required to spend time and money on outside advertising to lure customers in to their places of business as do owners of traditional

SURVIVING THE CRASH

A stock market crash in April 2000 made many eBay investors nervous. Despite the crash, though, its earnings were soaring. The number of users was up to nearly 16 million, an increase of 183 percent from the same period a year earlier. Item listings and sales had also doubled.

stores. Though some eBay sellers own shops, others are able to sell items from their homes, thereby eliminating the need to pay rent for a store space and cutting down on other expenses considerably.

BIG WIN IN COURT

In April 2001, eBay received a scare when a $100 million lawsuit was filed against the company on behalf of six individuals who purchased fake sports memorabilia on the site. In response, eBay argued that the site was merely a venue for sellers and that it was not responsible for the quality of the items sold on the site. The plaintiffs claimed eBay was a dealer and that by creating a category such as Sports: Autographs, it was confirming the authenticity of the autographs. A California state judge disagreed, however, siding with eBay and dismissing the suit in January 2001.

Meanwhile, the convenience for buyers is even greater. Not only can they shop at home, rather than driving their cars to stores, but they can also target the exact item they are seeking on one online site. And the auction system featured on eBay allows them to spend as much as they feel necessary to buy what is offered. Patrons can often buy an item for far less than can be purchased at an outside store.

Though eBay has continued to be easily the most successful online auction site, its impact has extended far beyond those who have used it to buy or sell items. The convenience of online shopping has resulted in its remarkable growth over the last decade. In addition, certain items proved to be an ideal fit for auction

Collectibles, such as American Civil War letters and memorabilia, proved well suited to the online auction marketplace of eBay.

sites, particularly eBay, which proved to be the most popular nearly from its inception. The popularity of eBay grew markedly due to the buying and selling of collectibles. The demand for children's toys, such as Beanie Babies, transformed eBay from a growing and popular site to an American phenomenon.

But profit had never been Omidyar's motivation. He yearned not only to give buyers and sellers an opportunity to work together online for a common purpose, but also to build a sense of community in which the users became friends as well as business partners. The problem was that those

WORDS FROM A GRADUATE

Invited to deliver the keynote address to the graduating students at alma mater Tufts University in 2002, Omidyar spoke about the values he used to create and grow eBay. He said,

In the deepest sense, eBay wasn't a hobby. And it wasn't a business. It was—and is—a community. . . .

I've come to see, in terms of my life, that community is the enduring interest of mine. From the earliest days at eBay, I posted five core values on the site. . . .

These are the five values I saw as essential: We believe people are basically good. We believe everyone has something to contribute. We believe that an honest, open environment can bring out the best in people. We recognize and respect everyone as a unique individual. We encourage you to treat others the way that you want to be treated. . . .

To understand that what today seems odd, unnecessary, off-beat—maybe even outrageous—may prove integral to solving tomorrow's problems. It's a matter of finding the connections that make community . . . and encouraging each individual to think from self to society to service.[1]

two goals counteracted one another. The more people streamed onto eBay, the less personal it became.

POWERFUL INFLUENCE

Omidyar had built an Internet giant through his idealism and desire to bring people together, but that success changed eBay forever. University of Purdue communications professor Josh Boyd noted the site's powerful influence in 2002:

Dozens of online auctions exist today selling everything from cigars to patents, but with every four million auctions at any one time and 42.4 million registered users, eBay is clearly the leader in the online auction business and arguably in any online business. It has consistently earned profits and has at times been the most visited shopping Website. Its success would not have happened had eBay not established a system that allowed people to feel safe enough to participate. How has eBay [established itself] as a safe and trustworthy place to do business? The answer is community. . . . Users trust each other and the system because they are all part of an "eBay community" in which they can feel safe.[2]

CONTINUED PROFITS

Well after eBay had ceased being a small, tight-knit community and Omidyar was no longer involved in the company, its income and profits continued to grow markedly. From 2006 to 2009, eBay's annual income more than doubled and its yearly profits increased substantially as well.

Whitman proved particularly successful as CEO of eBay. When she joined the company in 1998, it boasted $4.7 million revenues and 30 employees.

WHITMAN FOR GOVERNOR

Former eBay CEO Meg Whitman ran for governor of the state of California in 2010. The Republican Whitman lost the race, though, to Democrat Jerry Brown in the election for that office.

When she left in 2008, eBay had nearly $8 billion in revenues and 15,000 employees worldwide.

While eBay has attempted to maintain an eye to the future, buyers and sellers have changed their approach. According to current eBay CEO John Donahoe, who replaced Whitman in 2008, as recently as 2007 approximately 70 percent of all listings on the site were sold through auctions and approximately 30 percent were sold through fixed prices. In 2010, however, 45 percent of the items on eBay were open for bidding. Donahoe believed that fixed-price selling on the site could soar to 70 percent by the year 2011.

Only time will determine the accuracy of Donahoe's prediction. And though eBay has not only grown into one of the most influential and profitable sites on the Internet, its original basis for its success remains the same. Through the years it has maintained and earned a reputation for establishing trust between buyers and sellers. +

In September 2010, Donahoe spoke in China about
the future growth and partnerships of eBay.

The large corporate headquarters of eBay are
located in San Jose, California.

BEYOND EBAY

By the summer of 2000, Omidyar believed eBay
could thrive without him. He was also ready
and excited to accept new challenges in his
own life. So, though he kept the mostly honorary
title of chairman of the board, he left eBay.

He wasn't alone. Skoll, whom many consider a cofounder of the online auction site, also departed from the company. Both he and Omidyar sought to concentrate on their charitable efforts in the United States and around the world. Skoll also embarked on a career in fiction writing and movie production.

The tremendous growth of eBay had brought inevitable changes. The tight-knit community Omidyar had fostered had grown large and impersonal. Around 20 million users could now choose from a wide array of categories. The informal nature of the site he had started five years earlier was virtually gone—it was a victim of its own success. Public relations manager Mary Lou Song believed the turning point had been the move to sell eBay stock to the public. She said,

PARTICIPANT PRODUCTIONS

In 2002, several years after creating the Skoll Foundation, Jeff Skoll met movie producer Richard Barton Lewis at a dinner party. He asked Lewis why more films promoting activism were not being produced. Lewis replied that because of the high cost of making a movie, a studio could not afford to produce a flop.

Skoll had enough money to withstand a few flops, though. In 2005, he launched Participant Productions. The first four films it released were *Syriana, North Country, Murderball,* and *Good Night, and Good Luck*, which landed 11 Academy Award nominations. Participant Productions gained even greater success with *An Inconvenient Truth*, which helped raise awareness of the threat of global warming.

HELPING CANCER PATIENTS

One of the most interesting charitable projects Pam Omidyar pursued was a video game created for children with cancer. The game, called Re-Mission, allows kids to learn about their disease and medications while still having fun.

We really lived in la-la land with our community for two wonderful years, and it was the time of my life. But once you go public the pressures are completely different. You've got investors and analysts looking at you, you've got the media looking at you, you've got to worry about shares and stockholders and revenue.[1]

FAMILY AND PHILANTHROPY

The success of eBay had brought immense wealth to the Omidyar family. Yet, that wealth was not something that defined the Omidyars. Omidyar and wife Pam felt uneasy about residing in Silicon Valley. They believed something was wrong with a community when people such as teachers and policemen could not afford to live there. Omidyar was also a father now. He and Pam were busy raising their baby girl, the first of three children.

Through the Omidyar Foundation, the Omidyars had begun to spend some money on nonprofit organizations they deemed worthy. They were still looking for projects they felt would improve the lives of others. The Omidyars sought to give money to organizations that had proven to be successful or that showed a potential for success.

Their efforts were widespread. They provided funds for a program in Philadelphia in which elderly people work with toddlers. They gave $1 million to a community center in California with a food bank, housing agency, and health-care clinic all under one roof. They also endowed the Global Education Partnership, which sold crafts to support schools, with $165,000.

WANT TO BE A PHILANTHROPIST?

In November 2004, Omidyar became a major contributor to the DonorsChoose Web site. The site offers an opportunity for contributors to monitor the good work being done with their contribution. DonorsChoose allows people to give as little as $10 to a project posted by any schoolteacher who requires funding.

In 2003, one first-grade teacher in New York City, Cynthia Rosado, asked for nonfiction books her school district could not afford. In fact, not a single nonfiction book was available to her students, and they often lacked paper and pencils, as well. Rosado asked for $244 but ultimately received much more. Within a year, donors from 12 US states, Canada, and Australia funded 42 projects for her classroom. Because of the contributions made to DonorsChoose, Rosado's once barren classroom became as well equipped as any in a private school.

THE OMIDYAR NETWORK

The Omidyars came to believe that their philanthropy should not be limited just to nonprofit organizations. In large part because of the success of eBay, they realized that money-making businesses could also be effective agents of social change. To act on this realization, in 2004 they formed the Omidyar Network to provide funds to for-profit companies as well as nonprofit organizations. At the same time, they shut down their original charitable organization, the Omidyar Foundation.

The Omidyars now sought for-profit businesses whose goal was to make money in order to help people. Among them was Global Giving, which creates an online marketplace for nonprofits to match up with funders. The organization publishes a catalog of entrepreneurial projects in poor countries, such as a computer lab in rural Thailand and a crisis hotline for women in India. Global Giving founder and CEO Dennis Whittle expressed his appreciation for Omidyar and his selfless generosity. "What I like most about Pierre is that he's not about doing wild, wow things himself," Whittle said. "He's about enabling millions of people to do wow things themselves."[2]

Omidyar's charitable donations have benefited
Muhammad Yunus and the Grameen Bank.

Enabling people to do "wow" things also
attracted the Omidyars to Muhammad Yunus, who
earned the 2006 Nobel Prize in Economics. Yunus
invented microcredit and founded the Grameen
Bank. Microcredit is the providing of very small
loans (microloans) to poor people to enable them
to start businesses. It is part of a new concept called
microfinancing.

The Omidyars were excited to learn that
the Grameen Bank had been successful guiding
people out of poverty, including 1,152 women in
the African country of Uganda. Through money
provided by the Omidyars' donations to the

MEETUP

Omidyar's philanthropy has inspired many people. Among them is Scott Heiferman, who created the online social network Meetup. The purpose of Meetup is to bring together people with similar interests, hobbies, and causes. Omidyar was so impressed with Meetup that he invested in it through the Omidyar Network and became one of its directors. In 2006, eBay also stepped in and invested $2 million in the network.

Grameen Foundation, these women started their own businesses, such as selling wireless phone time to villagers. The money they earned allowed them to build homes and send children to school. The same formula allowed women in India to earn enough money selling their skills as computer instructors to earn a living wage within five months.

Most of the money provided to nonprofit organizations still came from the Omidyar Network, but the targets changed. The Omidyars focused on nonprofits that were already producing change and that were using the Internet as a tool to spread their messages. The Omidyars thought of the success of eBay and believed the same success could be achieved online by companies and organizations seeking to help others help themselves. +

Through his foundation, the Omidyar Network, Omidyar and his wife have enabled many people to improve their lives.

During a 2008 expo in Beijing, China, visitors browsed eBay's Web site.

THE FUTURE OF EBAY

While the Omidyars set out to give away billions of dollars, eBay went on a buying spree. The company continued to purchase online auction sites overseas and added classified advertising businesses to its list of acquisitions.

In 2002, eBay spent $1.5 billion for PayPal. It was deemed a natural fit because many eBay transactions are achieved through PayPal. The company had already acquired online auction sites in Germany, England, France, and South Korea. In 2003 it set its sights on a similar enterprise in China, purchasing EachNet for $150 million. A year later, eBay bought an online auction site in India for $50 million.

In 2004, eBay went to work wiping out online competition from classified ad businesses in the United States and elsewhere. One of its major acquisitions was approximately 25 percent of Craigslist, which has since grown rapidly in popularity. The purchase price was $32 million. Another major acquisition was Rent.com, for which eBay paid $415 million.

Its next step was ending competition from online shopping

EBAY LIVE

Not everything related to eBay is online. The site hosted a user convention called eBay Live every year from 2002 to 2008. The 2009 and 2010 events were canceled, but smaller workshops were held in various locations. Thousands of eBay users and fans, as well as hundreds of its employees, had flocked to eBay Live every year. The event has connected buyers, sellers, and others who have only known each other through the Internet.

sites. From 2005 to 2008, eBay bought in succession Shopping.com for $620 million, ticket agency StubHub for $310 million, and Bill Me Later for $1.2 billion. Meanwhile, eBay made its largest purchase ever in 2005 when it bought Skype, a Luxembourg-based Internet video phone service, for $2.6 billion.

As is expected when a string of high-prices purchases is made, some of them do not work out. Among them was Skype, which eBay sold 70 percent of the business in 2009 for $1.9 billion. The company admitted Skype was not a good fit for the online auction site.

BRIDGE TO EDUCATION

The Omidyar Network has invested in the Bridge International Academies, institutions that provide education to poor African children for less than four dollars a month and still manage to make a profit. According to the Omidyar Network, the successful schools can be used as models to educate students in other areas of the continent. With the Omidyar Network investment, Bridge International has pledged to provide high-quality, affordable education to more than 1 million children across Africa.

The first schools were built in the country of Kenya, but plans are to establish 1,800 schools in other areas of the continent by 2015. The institutions will not only provide education to children but also jobs for teachers and school administrators throughout Africa.

According to the Omidyar Network Web site, African children have historically not performed as well in testing as children from developed countries. In fact, African children have performed at only the third percentile, on average. It is the hope of those involved in Bridge International that the new educational system will thrive for years to come.

A DECADE OF CHANGE

The successes and failures of billion-dollar purchases certainly spoke volumes about how eBay had changed over a comparatively brief period. After all, it had been little more than a decade since Omidyar launched the free service on the Internet. He had little care for huge profits—his passion centered on an ability to bring people together and to help others.

With the Omidyar Network, Omidyar had continued to empower people. In 2009, he invested in Global Integrity, which gathers, creates, interprets, and distributes information on governments and corruption around the world. That year, Omidyar also put money into the Sunlight Foundation, which develops and supports technology that makes available information about Congress and the US government. He and others believe that more information about government activity should be made available and easily accessible to American people. With this knowledge, citizens are empowered to become more politically engaged and more knowledgeable voters.

The Omidyar Network's most far-reaching project, which began in 2009, was the funding of

GOING WIKI

In August 2009, the Omidyar Network announced it was providing a grant of up to $2 million over two years to the nonprofit Wikimedia Foundation. The group runs the online encyclopedia Wikipedia, one of the five most popular sites on the Internet. Despite the site's ad revenue, which comes from its estimated 300 million monthly visitors, it still requires outside money. The Wikimedia Foundation raised $6.2 million from 125,000 donors in one fund-raising drive at the end of 2008.

an organization called Ushahidi, a Swahili word that can be translated as "testimony." Ushahidi increases public awareness about various government actions around the world through reports from ordinary citizens. Its achievements have included the monitoring of elections in the Congo, India, and Mexico to make certain they were performed fairly and the tracking of medical supplies in various African nations.

GREAT GENEROSITY

Since being founded in 2004, the Omidyar Network has committed more than $300 million in investments and grants, including $169 million to nonprofit organizations. Omidyar has received tremendous help from his wife, Pam, who in 2005 launched Humanity United. It has worked to end atrocities such as the

Pam Omidyar, *right*, is involved with human rights issues and participated in the 2009 Freedom Awards with Dr. Kevin Bales of Free the Slaves.

mass slaughter of citizens in developing or warring nations. The ultimate goal is to achieve global peace.

Omidyar's mission has grown in scale, but the values that have driven that mission have not changed since that Labor Day weekend in 1995 when he launched an online auction site. Omidyar reiterated his beliefs in a short statement on the Omidyar Network Web site. It reads:

Because we are inspired by people's resourcefulness, ideas, and ability to address even the world's most challenging problems, we believe that no matter what their economic, social, or political starting point, people everywhere can be empowered to improve their own lives and the lives of those around them.[1]

The success of eBay has provided Omidyar opportunities to help many people around the world. Omidyar's original goal for his site was to provide a method for buyers and sellers to connect through an online community. It has since become an Internet phenomenon, exceeding Omidyar's expectations. Omidyar continues to achieve success through his charitable endeavors, all the while remaining true to his belief that the best way to help others is to provide them with opportunities to help themselves. +

Omidyar announced in 2010 that the Omidyar Network would set aside $55 million to fund technology that improves people's lives.

TIMELINE

1967	1984–1988	1988
Pierre Omidyar is born in Paris, France, on June 21.	Omidyar studies at Tufts University, earning a bachelor of science degree in computer science.	Omidyar lands an internship and then a full-time job at Innovative Data Design.

1996	1996	1996
Through stocks, Omidyar becomes a millionaire following the sale of eShop to Microsoft.	Omidyar launches the Feedback Forum in February and the Bulletin Board shortly afterward.	Jeff Skoll joins AuctionWeb and creates a business plan for the site.

1991	1994	1995
Omidyar and colleagues start the Ink Development Corporation. The business later becomes eShop.	Omidyar takes a position at General Magic.	Omidyar creates AuctionWeb on Labor Day weekend.

1997	1997	1998
In June, Benchmark Capital purchases 21.5 percent of AuctionWeb for $5 million.	In November, Omidyar embarks on the Fall Vision Tour to bring publicity to eBay.	In May, Meg Whitman accepts the position of CEO of eBay.

TIMELINE

1998	1998	2000
On September 24, an IPO results in the sale of $2 billion of eBay stock.	Omidyar becomes a billionaire and launches the Omidyar Foundation with wife Pam.	Omidyar leaves eBay, but remains chairman of the board. Skoll also leaves the company that year.

2004	2004	2005
eBay purchases approximately 25 percent of Craigslist for $32 million on August 13.	eBay buys Rent.com for $415 million on December 17.	eBay buys Skype for $2.6 billion.

2002

eBay purchases
PayPal for
$1.5 billion.

2003

eBay buys Chinese
auction site
EachNet.com for
$150 million.

2004

Omidyar creates the
Omidyar Network,
which provides
money for for-profit
organizations as
well as nonprofit
groups.

2005–2008

eBay acquires
Shopping.com,
StubHub, and Bill
Me Later.

2008

Meg Whitman
steps down as
CEO of eBay. John
Donahoe takes
her place.

2009

eBay sells 70
percent of Skype for
$1.9 billion.

ESSENTIAL FACTS

CREATOR

Pierre Omidyar, June 21, 1967

DATE LAUNCHED

1995

CHALLENGES

The site crashed several times, which disconnected users from eBay for long periods of time. A major crash in 1999 lasted 22 hours and cost eBay significant revenue from both customers and stockholders. Disputes also arose between buyers and sellers. These disputes eventually dissipated through the use of the Feedback Forum and rating system on the site.

SUCCESSES

Omidyar founded the first highly successful online auction site on Labor Day Weekend in 1995 and called it AuctionWeb. The site was later named eBay. It became particularly useful for buying and selling collectibles, such as Beanie Babies. From the late 1990s to early 2000s, eBay acquired or created auction Web sites in countries around the world, making eBay a global presence. Omidyar became one of the richest entrepreneurs in the United States because of his creation of eBay.

IMPACT ON SOCIETY

The eBay site has provided convenience for sellers by allowing them to sell items from their homes, which eliminates the need to pay rent for a place of business, cuts down on other expenses, and eliminates the need for advertising. The convenience for buyers is that they can shop at home and target the exact item they are seeking. Often, customers can buy items for far less than can be purchased at a store. The number of people making purchases through the Internet has grown, at least partly due to the influence of eBay. The popularity of eBay grew markedly due to the buying and selling of collectibles.

QUOTE

"If you're passionate about something and you work hard, then I think you'll be successful. If you start a business because you think you're going to make a lot of money at it, then you probably won't be successful, because that's the wrong reason to start a business. You have to really believe in what you're doing, be passionate about it so that you will put in the hours and the hard work that it takes to actually succeed there, and then you'll be successful."
—*Pierre Omidyar*

GLOSSARY

auction

A sale of an item in which bids are cast with the highest bidder gaining possession of that item.

chief executive officer

The working head of an organization or business, also called the CEO.

collectible

An item that is collected and which may increase in value.

commerce

Buying and selling of goods or services.

donor

An individual who gives money to a charity or organization.

empower

To help people help themselves.

hardware

The physical parts of a computer.

initial public offering

The first selling of stock of a particular business to the public, also called IPO.

Internet

The computer network that connects smaller computer networks and organizational computer facilities from around the world.

invest

To purchase part of a business with the intention of making money as the business grows in value.

libertarian

A person who favors the notion of free will and individual rights and freedom.

nonprofit

An organization established not for the purpose of making a profit.

philanthropy

The philosophy and act of selflessly providing money to those deemed less fortunate.

revenue

The total income of a company or individual.

software

Programs used to direct the operation of a computer.

stock

Shares owned of a particular company.

venture capitalist

An individual who provides money for newly formed businesses with the intention of making money as the business grows in value.

ADDITIONAL RESOURCES

SELECTED BIBLIOGRAPHY

Cohen, Adam. *The Perfect Store: Inside eBay*. New York: Little, 2002. Print.

"Pierre Omidyar Interview." *Academy of Achievement Online*. Academy of Achievement, 27 Oct. 2000. Web.

Stross, Randall E. *eBoys: The First Inside Account of Venture Capitalists at Work*. New York: Crown, 2000. Print.

FURTHER READINGS

Griffith, Jim. *The Official eBay Bible*. Rev. ed. New York: Gotham, 2007. Print.

Horvitz, Leslie Alan. *Meg Whitman: President and CEO of eBay*. New York: Ferguson, 2006. Print.

Woog, Adam. *Pierre M. Omidyar: Creator of eBay*. Detroit, MI: KidHaven, 2008. Print.

WEB LINKS

To learn more about eBay, visit ABDO Publishing Company online at **www.abdopublishing.com**. Web sites about eBay are featured on our Book Links page. These links are routinely monitored and updated to provide the most current information available.

PLACES TO VISIT

Computer History Museum
1401 N. Shoreline Blvd., Mountain View, CA 94043
650-810-1010
http://www.computerhistory.org/internet_history
This museum explores the history of computers from 1962 to
the present. It also features various exhibits, including one about
Charles Babbage, who designed the first computer engine in 1849.

Strong National Museum of Play
One Manhattan Square, Rochester, NY 14607
585-263-2700
http://www.museumofplay.org
Dedicated to the study and exploration of play, this museum
holds collections of historical materials related to play. In its Toy
Manufacturers Collections, the museum includes 800 examples of
Beanie Babies, the toy that jump-started eBay's success.

The Tech Museum
201 South Market Street, San Jose, CA 95113
408-294-8324
http://www.thetech.org
With hundreds of exhibits, this museum strives to provide science
and technology experiences to its visitors. The museum includes a
gallery of the technological innovations created in Silicon Valley.

SOURCE NOTES

CHAPTER 1. BIRTH OF A GIANT

1. "Interview: Pierre Omidyar." *Academy of Achievement Online.*
Academy of Achievement, 27 Oct. 2000. Web. 26 Dec. 2009.
2. Ibid.
3. Adam Cohen. *The Perfect Store.* New York: Little, 2002.
Print. 22.

CHAPTER 2. NOT JUST ANOTHER KID

1. "Interview: Pierre Omidyar." *Academy of Achievement Online.*
Academy of Achievement, 27 Oct. 2000. Web. 26 Dec. 2009.
2. Ibid.
3. Michelle Conlin. "Online Extra: A Talk with Pierre
Omidyar." *BusinessWeek Online.* BusinessWeek, 29 Nov. 2004.
Web. 31 Jan. 2010.
4. "Interview: Pierre Omidyar." *Academy of Achievement Online.*
Academy of Achievement, 27 Oct. 2000. Web. 26 Dec. 2009.

CHAPTER 3. INTO THE REAL WORLD

1. Randall E. Stross. *eBoys.* New York: Crown, 2000. Print. 52.
2. Pierre Omidyar. "Founder's Letter." *ebay.com.* eBay, 26 Feb.
1996. Web. 8 Nov. 2010.
3. "Interview: Pierre Omidyar." *Academy of Achievement Online.*
Academy of Achievement, 27 Oct. 2000. Web. 26 Dec. 2009.

CHAPTER 4. NEW TALENT AND NEW INVESTORS

1. Adam Cohen. *The Perfect Store*. New York: Little, 2002. Print. 31.

CHAPTER 5. THE GREAT EBAY FLOOD

1. "Interview: Pierre Omidyar." *Academy of Achievement Online*. Academy of Achievement, 27 Oct. 2000. Web. 26 Dec. 2009.

2. Michelle Conlin. "Online Extra: A Talk with Pierre Omidyar." *BusinessWeek Online*. BusinessWeek, 29 Nov. 2004. Web. 31 Jan. 2010.

CHAPTER 6. A NEW CEO AND PHILANTHROPY

1. Randall E. Stross. *eBoys*. New York: Crown, 2000. Print. 57.

2. Quentin Hardy. "The Radical Philanthropist." *Forbes Online*. Forbes, 1 May 2000. Web. 8 Feb. 2010.

CHAPTER 7. PROSPERITY, GIVING, AND A SETBACK

1. "Interview: Pierre Omidyar." *Academy of Achievement Online*. Academy of Achievement, 27 Oct. 2000. Web. 26 Dec. 2009.

SOURCE NOTES CONTINUED

CHAPTER 8. THE EBAY LEGACY

1. Pierre Omidyar and Pam Omidyar. "From Self to Society: Citizenship to Community for a World of Change." *enews.tufts.edu.* Tufts e-news, 19 May 2002. Web. 9 Feb. 2010.

2. Josh Boyd. "In Community We Trust: Online Security Communication at eBay." *jcmc.indiana.edu.* Journal of Computer-Mediated Communication, Apr. 2002. Web. 26 Oct. 2010.

CHAPTER 9. BEYOND EBAY

1. Adam Cohen. *The Perfect Store.* New York: Little, 2002. Print. 305.

2. Michelle Conlin and Rob Hof. "The eBay Way: The site's founder wanted to know how best to give. He asked, he listened. Here's what he learned." *BusinessWeek Online.* BusinessWeek, 29 Nov. 2004. Web. 9 Feb. 2010.

CHAPTER 10. THE FUTURE OF EBAY

1. "Evolution." *omidyar.com.* Omidyar Network, n.d. Web. 11 Feb. 2010.

INDEX

INDEX CONTINUED

ABOUT THE AUTHOR

Martin Gitlin is a freelance writer based in Cleveland, Ohio. He has written more than 25 educational books. Gitlin has won more than 45 awards during his 25 years as a writer, including first place for general excellence from the Associated Press.

PHOTO CREDITS

Jb Reed/Bloomberg/Getty Images, cover, 87; Acey Harper/Time Life Pictures/Getty Images, 6, 96; Anke van Wyk/Shutterstock Images, 11, 97 (top); Robert Levin/Corbis, 13; Shutterstock Images, 14, 18, 62, 72, 98 (bottom); Kevin D. Walsh/Shutterstock Images, 21; Charles O'Rear/Corbis, 22; Frith's Photography/ Bigstock, 24; Kim Kulish/Corbis, 31; Mark Savage/Corbis, 32; Damian Dovarganes/AP Images, 37; John Harding/Time Life Pictures/Getty Images, 41; The Pueblo Chieftain, Kristi Guerrero/ AP Images, 42; Sebastiao Moreira/Corbis, 44; Nathaniel Welch/ Corbis, 51; Paul Sakuma/AP Images, 52, 97 (bottom); Ames D. Wilson/Liaison Agency/Getty Images, 55; Tom Williams/Roll Call/ Getty Images, 59; PRNewsFoto/Chrysler LLC, Tom Strickland/ AP Images, 61; Joerg Sarbach/AP Images, 64; Keith Dannemiller/ Corbis, 71; Sun Journal, Jose Leiva/AP Images, 75; Imaginechina via AP Images/AP Images, 79, 88, 99; Proehl Studios/Corbis, 80; Sipa via AP Images/AP Images, 85; Mark Sullivan/Getty Images, 93, 98 (top); Andrew Harrer/Bloomberg/Getty Images, 95